Six Eucharistic Prayers as Proposed in 1996

The Official Texts for Final Approval with Introduction and Commentary

by

Colin Buchanan

Vicar, St Mark's, Gillingham, Kent
Hon Asst Bishop, Diocese of Rochester
Member of Revision Committee on Eucharistic Prayers 1995

and

Trevor Lloyd

Archdeacon of Barnstaple
Vice-Chairman of Liturgical Commission
Chairman of Steering Committee on Eucharistic Prayers 1995

GROVE BOOKS LIMITED
RIDLEY HALL RD CAMBRIDGE CB3 9HU

Contents

Note

The actual proposals of the Revision Committee, marginally amended by the House of Bishops, ran beyond the text of the Six Eucharistic Prayers, and included a redrafted Opening Note 13 to Rite A about Proper Prefaces, a simplified 'Preparation of the Gifts' (section 32), alternative Acclamations for existing Eucharistic Prayers and alternative words of distribution. These have been omitted here for reasons of space, confining this Booklet to the Eucharistic Prayers alone. The addition to Note 13 would have applied to the new Eucharistic Prayers as well as to the old and ran as follows: *'On special occasions, other Proper Prefaces or Insertions may be used at the points indicated in the prayer. These should be selected from authorized or commended sources or may be composed for a single occasion.'*

The Annex to GS1120 entitled 'Eucharists when Children are Present' is published here in a very slightly shortened form, as the Revision Committee in 1995 recommended that the Annex should be published with the texts.

Legal Note

The publication of these prayers does not directly or indirectly imply that they can be regarded as authorized for use in churches.

The Cover Illustration is Self-explanatory

First Impression April 1996

ISSN 0144-1728

ISBN 1 85174 313 8

1
Introduction

On 13 and 14 February 1996, for the first time in over sixteen years, the General Synod of the Church of England voted on a motion to give Final Approval to six new eucharistic prayers. To our deep regret, the House of Laity of the Synod failed to give the prayers the two-thirds majority needed for authorization, and they were accordingly defeated. We two were planning to write a Grove Booklet to introduce and commend these prayers when they authorized, and much of this Booklet was already drafted. In the event it is a somewhat different publication to which we have given our hand. It is different in that we cannot now make suggestions about their use, or about ways in which their use should be monitored and evaluated. That happy prospect has disappeared. But the Booklet is also different in that we are able to publish the prayers themselves in the form in which they came to the Synod for Final Approval—a publishing bonus which had not been in prospect before. It would in fact have been difficult for the official publishers to have published and promoted the six prayers, once their lords and masters in Synod had rejected them. Church House Publishing has, however, been extremely helpful to this unofficial publication, and we have gratefully received from them the text of the six prayers, with their 'proper' insertions, and we here display them in the centre pages of the Booklet for the sake of later study, comparison and research, and even for use in whatever places—in England or elsewhere—it may be lawful or at least possible so to do. We have a sense of doing what the House of Bishops themselves did in 1929, when it was the House of Commons which had defeated *their* Book. They found ways in which the Book could be published, and, when it was published, they drafted a legal health warning on its fly leaves, reprinted on page 2 opposite. We echo that warning and have modelled the title of this Booklet on the title of their Book.

New eucharistic texts, that is, 'alternative services,' for the Church of England began with Series 1 (the old 'interim rite') in 1966, and Series 2 (the first new writing) in 1967. In the processes from 1964, when the first drafting of Series 2 was begun on the Commission, to 1980, when Rite A gave middle-term stability, close interest in the rite focused on the text of the eucharistic prayer—and there was only one eucharistic prayer per rite until Rite A emerged with four. The stages of development of these prayers ran as follows.

Series 2

The Commission provided a draft prayer based largely upon the text of Hippolytus. Colin Buchanan dissented in 1966 over the offering of the bread and cup to God in the anamnesis paragraph. The House of Laity insisted a single unitive way forward be found, and a compromise text ('we make the memorial') was agreed. The amended text was authorized (with hardly any dissent) from September 1967, and is to be found to this day (slightly adjusted) in the second 'Thanksgiving' in Rite B in the *ASB* (pp 193-5). The sense of relief at finding a text almost all could use was almost audible.

In the process, the English language used was still in 'thou'-form; the eucharistic prayer though longer than that in the *BCP* remained a monologue, without congregational responses between the Sanctus and the 'Amen;' and two manual acts remained in the margin of the narrative of institution. There was no provision for supplementary consecration.

Series 3

The great change from Series 2 to Series 3 was the substitution of 'you' for 'thou' with a consequent alteration in the whole character of the English language used. In the eucharistic prayer the structure and general character remained identifiable, but there were changes made both from Series 2 to the 1971 initial draft and from that draft to the finally authorized form in 1973. The following changes of some substance should be noted.

(a) a much greater provision for proper prefaces;
(b) an inclusion of 'by the power of your Holy Spirit' in the epiclesis;
(c) the deletion from the narrative of institution of indented rubrics prescribing manual acts;
(d) the addition of acclamations after the narrative of institution;
(e) a strengthening of the references to Christ's death as being his sacrifice in the anamnesis;
(f) a rewording of the petition for fruitful reception (or 'second epiclesis');
(g) the addition of a congregational doxology leading in to the 'Amen'—'Blessing and honour...'
(h) the finding of a form for supplementary consecration.

The text was, however, still clearly of the Hippolytan family.

Rite A

After the Worship and Doctrine Measure came into force on 1 September 1975, the Synod resolved to produce a substantial service book, and the Commission put out 28,000 questionnaires on Series 3, and began the task of revising the text in the light of use and comment. After the first stage in Synod the Revision Committee had to handle over 1000 would-be amendments from members of Synod, a good proportion of which related to the eucharistic prayers. Two were brought from an appendix to join in the main text the lightly retouched eucharistic prayer of Series 3—and a fourth prayer came by a sidewind into the Committee, a prayer more closely related to Hippolytus than any previous one had been. This was retouched also, and inserted into the alternatives as the 'Third Eucharistic Prayer.' A 'Pattern following the Order of the *Book of Common Prayer*' was also now set out in full, though (because of the overall *BCP* structure) it was not amenable to being put in parallel to the other four prayers, and it became part of a completely separate alternative order for the second half of the service; an unexpected 'Eucharistic Prayer for use with the Sick' also appeared—in an appendix.

The texts were subjected to a lengthy revision process in Synod, and were finally approved in November 1979, to be used from 1 May 1980, and then to appear within the *ASB* from November 1980. There was again virtually no opposition recorded in the debates or the votes. For almost the first time the Church of England now had alternative eucharistic prayers within one rite; and all had been drafted on the principle that every text must be usable by all strands of Anglican thought and spirituality, and that none should be of sectional interest only. All were 'pre-inclusive' (like the rest of the *ASB*) in their terminology. And, although the First and Third Prayers are probably clear favourites, all four have passed into regular use. These four have been the standard fare of the Church of England for a decade and a half at the time of writing. One of the pressures behind the production of the new six was the sense that there was a considerable sameness in the four prayers of Rite A.

The whole *ASB* was authorized for use until 31 December 1990, and in the mid-1980s this licence was extended to 31 December 2000 (the end of the millennium to all numerate observers). At the time we write, it has therefore passed the three-quarters stage in its shelf-life, and is clearly entering into its last stages of not only legality but also credibility. The six defeated prayers were in the forefront of the programme for new liturgical texts for the period following 31 December 2000. It remains to be seen whether a credible timetable, for getting a full range of material, well tried and suitably revised, into place in time for that watershed date, can now be recreated and closely followed.

That, however, is another exercise. The current one is more simply a setting out of the genesis and growth of the six, a republishing of them for the record, and a reproducing with them of the material, to be found here in chapter 5, which the Liturgical Commission wrote in 1994, and the Revision Committee recommended in 1995 should be included in all printings of the texts, 'Eucharists for use when Children are Present.' The two of us have stood close to the process. We were both on the Revision Committee of Synod which in May 1995 fixed the actual number at six and proposed to Synod the texts in their virtually final form. Trevor Lloyd was of course also a senior member of the Liturgical Commission which took responsibility for earlier forms of the prayers and brought them to the House of Bishops, and he was the chairman of the Steering Committee which did the drafting and redrafting of the texts within the Revision Committee—and Colin Buchanan, who had once chaired the Steering Committee for Rite A, returned to Synod as a member of the House of Bishops from October 1990, and was present at each of the meetings of that House to which reference is made below. Out of our combined experience and our separate judgments about the needs of the Church of England today, we do the only positive service to the six texts now open to us to do: we publish them.

2
Principles of the New Eucharistic Prayers

Four members of the Liturgical Commission began work on new eucharistic prayers in 1986, seeking to provide better forms for use in urban priority areas and also for use where whole families are together at the eucharist. Drafts were tried out and refined and sent to the House of Bishops, before four were published in 'Rite C' in the 1989, *Patterns for Worship*. The report had a short commentary on each and an outline of the general principles followed, including:

> '3. There should be a Trinitarian balance within a eucharistic prayer, but not necessarily a Trinitarian pattern. Nor is there any need...for the thanksgiving to be a credal historical list...The Church should be encouraged to rejoice in the contemporary effects of the historic facts...
> 4. We believe there should be some texts available which are thoroughly responsive [not only eliminating monologues but also embodying] our belief that the whole congregation is involved in celebrating the eucharist.
> 5. "Consecration" is by the whole prayer and action of the community, and cannot be identified with particular words or a particular stage in the prayer...[as a matter of historical judgment] the narrative [of institution] is regarded as a later insertion...in a sequence of thanksgiving and supplication. [We have a different form of the narrative in each prayer.]'

1. Structure, the Trinity and the Spirit

The Commission's 'recipe' for a eucharistic prayer looked like this:

> 'A eucharistic prayer, whether it takes the form of extended monologue with acclamations, or a dialogue between president and congregation, normally includes the following:
> - thanksgiving for creation, redemption and the work of the Spirit
> - the memorial prayer for the church to receive and grow in the life of Christ
> - doxology, offering praise to God the Holy Trinity.
>
> These are the "deep structures" of the prayer and they need to be clear in the shape of the ideas expressed within them...
> The pattern of the prayer is normally
> - an opening dialogue
> - an introduction to praise
> - an extended act of thanksgiving
> - the narrative of institution
> - the memorial prayer
> - the prayer for the blessing of the Spirit' (*Patterns for Worship*, p 28)'

The above principles together provide a Trinitarian shape. This was wholly overt as the position of the Commission in 1989, but was almost totally overlooked in discussion until Trevor Lloyd introduced the Bishops' choice of texts to Synod in November 1994. Then in his opening speech he pointed out how Rite A's Hippolytan ground-plan obscures the Trinitarian structure,
(a) by locating the institution narrative within what is actually supplication, rather than as a climax of Christ-centred praise; and
(b) by the concomitant placing of the invocation of the Spirit before the narrative as though preparing for a 'precatory' concept of consecration.
A Trinitarian structure could of course be provided in a variety of ways and with all manner of adroit complexities. But the Commission was exploring whether a degree of simplicity would help educate people in using the eucharistic prayers; and a grasp of the underlying structures in one or two prayers should not only enable them to enter easily into the spiritual action when those prayers are used, but should also do the same with other prayers also. Thus, for instance, it was decided not only to put the weight of invocation into the section focusing on the Spirit, but also to abandon any idea of an earlier epiclesis altogether. Similarly the Commission found no problem in addressing prayer and praise to all three persons of the Trinity by name, provided that the person of the Godhead addressed was actually focal in that particular section of the prayer.

2. Accessibility, Language, Culture and Responses

The prayers here which come from the original 'Rite C' (viz, nos 2,3,4 and part of 5) reflect something of the 'UPA' and 'family' background, though the Commission never let them be treated as exclusively for certain groups. The joint group which drafted prayer 5 (for use when children are present) agreed:

> 'Such a prayer must be suitable for the whole church...It is potentially divisive to have a Eucharistic Prayer for just one group of people...'

They went on to echo the Commission's principles on language:

> 'The language should be vivid, creative, evocative, pictorial, and not too cerebral, conceptual or "theological," or expressed in complicated constructions, such that sentences ramble on with many dependent clauses...'

They also distinguish between various kinds of congregational responding:

> '[The sense of being short or long lies not so much in the actual length of a prayer] it is the length of individual monologue which is more difficult for children. Some people find that where the presidential words are broken up with a series of responses, the prayer can be longer. These responses can be of two sorts...the short repeated phrase...[and] the longer response which contributes to the action of the prayer. [But there are also difficulties

about longer responses—including needing a text open to be read.]...'

The Commission accordingly drafted prayers with different kinds of responses:

In prayer 1 the president's 'we praise you' is answered by the congregation's 'Hosanna in the highest' in the first part of the prayer, concluding with the traditional 'Hosanna' in the Sanctus and Benedictus; in the second and third parts, touching on the work of the Son and the Spirit, the president's 'we thank you' is answered by the congregation's 'We praise your holy name.'

In prayer 2 the main interest centres more on the three separate variable insertions which give a great seasonal and thematic range of choices to the prayer. If, however, the note is followed which allows the regular repetition of 'To you be glory and praise for ever!', then the prayer becomes a majestic burst of congregational praise.

In prayer 3 there are three different kinds of response: firstly, a careful redrafting and relocating into the prayer itself of 'offertory' prayers sometimes used separately before the taking of the bread and cup; secondly, longish anthems from the heavenly worship in the Book of Revelation; and, thirdly, a congregational invocation of the Spirit.

The responses in prayer 4 vary and need following carefully unless they are by design simply repeated after the president; and they highlight and reinforce the Trinitarian structure of the prayer in their addressing in turn the different persons of the Godhead.

In prayer 5 the Rite A responses are used in the non-variable parts, and the suggestions in the appendix about the creating of responsive prefaces indicate how a single line, learned once and then repeated by heart, will well serve the style of the prayer.

In prayer 6 the first prayer in Rite A has been shortened and the congregation's responses enriched with more, but well-known, acclamations.

3. Consecration, Sacrifice, the Cross and the Spirit

Despite the wide variety of themes found when all six prayers are put together, at the heart of each of them is the mystery of the sacrifice of Christ on the cross, usually especially singled out from the other mighty acts of God. In many cases this is more explicit than it was in Rite A. The Commission was conscious of two problems to solve; and the first of these was how to relate Christ's death on the cross to the present event of celebration. An inspection of the texts of the anamnesis from prayers 2,3 and 4 will illustrate the different ways the Commission explored, and we may compare these with other statements about the cross in the same prayers.

The Commission itself thought that the narrative of institution might be employed in various ways to add weight to the doctrine of the atonement in the rite. In the event the Revision Committee went some way to standardizing the texts and the House of Bishops completed the process. Only prayer 5 escaped the straitjacket.

3
Progress to Defeat

The Liturgical Commission published 'Rite C' in *Patterns for Worship*, in November 1989. General Synod debated it in February 1990, and the House of Bishops, which has to introduce liturgy into Synod, then asked the Commission to edit the eucharistic material for Synod: *A Service of the Word*. was authorized separately. In November 1991 the Synod asked for 'Eucharistic Prayers suitable for use...at services with children present.' This coloured all discussion of eucharistic prayers thereafter.

The Commission brought eucharistic material to the Bishops in January 1992 but their packet was sent back, and the need of prayers for use with children was added to the brief. They returned in January 1994 with *five* eucharistic prayers, but still none 'for use when children are present.' The House hesitated, and sent the texts to Synod in GS1120 asking if Synod *wanted* to begin the authorization process. The Synod amended their motion and asked the House, '...to introduce eucharistic proposals, including up to five Eucharistic Prayers, at least one...for use with children present...'

The Bishops in October 1994 reduced the five prayers to two, and sent them to Synod with a note that neither was 'for use when children are present,' but not explaining why, instead of five, there were only two, nor why these two in particular. Trevor Lloyd, as chairman of the Steering Committee, moved 'General Approval' in Synod on 30 November 1994. He set out liturgical principles (see chapter 2 above); and he dropped hints that he was unhappy with reducing the number of prayers to two. The Synod duly approved, and the prayers were referred to the Revision Committee (on which the present editors sat).

Only 14 Synod members made submissions, some about drafting points, some restoring the other prayers. We strengthened the references to the atoning death of Christ and to the depths of sin; we partly standardized the narrative of institution; we softened the invoking of the Holy Spirit on the elements (rather than on the action); and we tightened language and enhanced some imagery. Thus amended we adopted four of the five prayers in GS1120; added a fifth for use with children; and wrote a sixth in some continuity with Rite A (though in a more responsive form). We endorsed he total number and forwarded the texts for the Revision Stage in Synod in July 1995—and at that there were *no* motions to have the texts amended, though the Bishops gave hints that they might reduce the number at the last stage. In fact both in October 1995 and in January 1996 they made very minor changes, without touching the total number, and returned the prayers to Synod.

On 13-14 February 1996 the Synod debated 'Final Approval.' The voting, requiring a two-thirds majority in each House, was: Bishops 25-10: Clergy 164-44: Laity 135-81. And that was that. For the first time liturgical texts had been rejected in Synod without anyone knowing what was determinative in that defeat.

4
The Eucharistic Prayers

EUCHARISTIC PRAYER 1

The Lord be with you **and also with you.**	*or*	The Lord is here. **His Spirit is with us.**

Lift up your hearts.
We lift them to the Lord.

Let us give thanks to the Lord our God.
It is right to give him thanks and praise.

God our Father, giver of life and light,
maker of all things,

*We praise you for the earth and sea, for wind and fire.
*We thank you for the peoples of the world.

For all the wonder of creation we praise you:
Hosanna in the highest!

*You made our hearts to share your love.
*You know our tears and laughter.

For your gift of love we praise you:
Hosanna in the highest!

Therefore with all your people of every place and age
we join the saints and angels
in songs of everlasting praise:
Holy, holy, holy Lord,
God of power and might,
Heaven and earth are full of your glory.
Hosanna in the highest!

(Blessed is he who comes in the name of the Lord.
Hosanna in the highest!)

Father, you love us so much
that you gave your Son, born of Mary,
to live among us and to die rejected on the cross.
You raised him to life, victorious over sin,
to reign with you for ever.

For your gift of Christ we thank you:
We praise your holy name.

Note *The lines with asterisks may be replaced by alternative insertions of similar length*

At table with his friends
on the night before he died
Jesus took bread and gave you thanks.
He broke it and gave it to them, saying:
'Take, eat. This is my body, given for you.'

At the end of supper, taking the cup of wine,
he gave you thanks, and said:
'Drink this, all of you;
This is my blood of the new covenant,
shed for you and for many for the forgiveness of sins.
Do this in remembrance of me.'

For the sacrifice of Christ we thank you:
We praise your holy name.

So now we do this to obey your Son's command.
We stand before you with this bread and cup,
and proclaim the Lord's death until he comes again.
We praise you for Jesus our living Lord:
He is the one true sacrifice who brings us peace with you.

For our life in Christ we thank you:
We praise your holy name.

Through him, risen and ascended,
you send your Spirit
to bring new life to your world.
Pour your Holy Spirit on us now,
as we feed on the body and blood of Christ,
and live and grow in him.

For your gift of the Spirit we thank you:
We praise your holy name.

Unite us around this table
with your whole church in earth and heaven.
Bring us to feast in your eternal kingdom,
with (*N* and) all who live in Christ.
Transformed by your Spirit we shall rejoice with them,
and sing your praise, Father almighty, for ever.
Alleluia!
Salvation and glory and power belong to our God.
Amen. Alleluia.

(or in Lent -
Worthy is the lamb who was slain,
To receive power and wealth, wisdom and strength,
honour and glory and praise. Amen.)

EUCHARISTIC PRAYER 2

The Lord be with you *or* The Lord is here.
and also with you. **His Spirit is with us.**

Lift up your hearts.
We lift them to the Lord.

Let us give thanks to the Lord our God.
It is right to give him thanks and praise.

Blessed are you, Lord God, our light and our salvation;
to you be glory and praise for ever!
From the beginning you have created all things
and all your works echo the silent music of your praise.
You make us in your image to reflect your glory.

You give us breath and speech
that with all the powers of heaven
we may find a voice to sing your praise:
Holy, holy, holy Lord,
God of power and might,
Heaven and earth are full of your glory.
Hosanna in the highest!

(Blessed is he who comes in the name of the Lord.
Hosanna in the highest!)

How wonderful the work of your hands, O Lord!
As a mother tenderly gathers her children
you embraced a people as your own...*

Insertions (a) optional here

From them you raised up Jesus, our Saviour,
the living bread, in whom all hungers are satisfied...*

Insertions (b) optional here

In the upper room with his friends
on the night before he died,
Jesus took bread and gave you thanks.
He broke it and gave it to them, saying:
Take, eat. This is my body, given for you.'

At the end of supper, taking the cup of wine,
he gave you thanks, and said:
'Drink this, all of you;
This is my blood of the new covenant,

* ***to you be glory and praise for ever!*** *may be repeated as an Acclamation after each of the asterisked lines*

shed for you and for many for the forgiveness of sins.
Do this in remembrance of me.'*

Great is the mystery of faith:
Christ has died:
Christ is risen:
Christ will come again.

Father, we plead with confidence
his sacrifice made once for all upon the cross;
we remember his dying and rising in glory,
and we rejoice that he prays for us at your right hand:

Pour out your Holy Spirit
as we bring before you these gifts from your own creation,
that they may be for us the body and blood of your dear Son...*

Insertions (c) optional here

By him, with him, and in him,
with all who stand before you in earth and heaven,
we worship you, Father almighty,
in songs of everlasting praise:

Blessing and honour and glory and power
be yours for ever and ever. Amen.

OPTIONAL INSERTIONS

1 Ferial

(a) You filled them with longing for a peace without fear,
a justice that would never fail.

(b) He offered his life for sinners,
and with a love stronger than death
he opened wide his arms on the cross.

(c) May we who eat and drink in his presence
be constant in prayer and strong in love
until all creation is made one in Christ.

2 The Kingdom, Advent

(a) You spoke to them through prophets
who looked for the day of deliverance to draw near.

(b) He came among us as your servant,
to be Emmanuel, your presence with us.

(c) Gather your Church from the ends of the earth into your Kingdom,
that we, with all your people,
may share in Christ's eternal banquet.

3 Incarnation

(a) You taught them to hope for salvation,
the joy of every longing heart.

(b) He was born in the poverty of a stable,
to make known the riches of your Kingdom.

(c) As we break this bread and share this cup,
may we know the presence of your
Word made flesh.

4 Baptism

(a) You called them in covenant
to be a light to all the nations.

(b) Through him we are saved for ever
and born again to righteousness.

(c) By the baptism of water and
your Holy Spirit
may we witness to your truth
in all the world
until he comes in final victory.

and/or

Remember your Church in every land,
redeemed by the blood of your Christ.
Reveal her unity, guard her faith,
and preserve her in peace.
Remember all who minister in your Church...
Remember those baptised today...
...in Christ Jesus our Lord.

5 Candlemas

(a) In worship and sacrifice they drew near,
entering your gates with thanksgiving.

(b) Brought to the temple in his mother's arms,
he was proclaimed as the light of all the nations.

(c) As by your Spirit he was welcomed with joy by Anna and Simeon,
so may we and all your people rejoice in your presence
and be changed from glory to glory.

6 Penitence

(a) Again and again you forgave them
and restored them to your love.

(b) By his death he broke the power of sin
and made us holy through his blood.

(c) At this table make us one in Christ;
open to us a new and living way into your presence.

7 The Cross, Passiontide

(a) When they turned away and rebelled
your love remained steadfast.

(b) For our sins he was lifted up
that he might draw the whole world to himself.

(c) Unite in his cross
all who share the food and drink
of his new unending life.

8 Resurrection

(a) You delivered them from slavery
and brought them to the promised land.

(b) By his victory over the grave
he burst the gates of death for ever.

(c) Shine through the darkness of our doubt and sorrow
that the light of his risen presence
may brighten the path before us.

9 Bread of Life

(a) You fed them with manna in the wilderness
as they walked the pilgrim path in your sight.

(b) He broke bread with those whom others scorned
and when the multitude were hungry
he fed them abundantly.

(c) Make us one body, a holy and living sacrifice,
to serve you acceptably as a royal priesthood.

10 The Vine

(a) You planted them as your own choice vine,
but again and again they turned from you in sin.

(b) He is the true vine, your chosen one,
in whom we are joined to bear fruit in plenty.

(c) As we taste and see that the Lord is gracious,
may we dwell in him, as he lives in us.

11 The Spirit

(a) You promised to pour upon them your Holy Spirit,
that the young might see visions
and the old have dreams of your coming Kingdom.

(b) He breathed upon his disciples the power of your Spirit
to proclaim the good news to all peoples.

(c) Renew the life of your Spirit
in all who share Christ's eucharistic feast.

12 Trinity

(a) To them you revealed the glory of your Godhead
as they ate and drank in your presence.

(b) At the River Jordan,
you declared him your beloved Son,
baptising him in the power of the Spirit.

(c) By these holy mysteries enfold us in the love
which you have revealed in your Son and in the Holy Spirit.
May we find mercy and grace in communion with all your saints
in Christ Jesus for ever.

13 City

(a) You gave them the hope of a city
the place of unity and peace.

(b) He gave up his life outside the city gate
and opened for all the way to heaven.

(c) Dwell among us as we journey
to the new Jerusalem to be your people,
where our God reigns for ever in Christ.

14 The Saints

(a) You made them a holy nation
and brought them home victorious.

(b) In him you have received us as your sons and daughters
and made us citizens of your Kingdom.

14 The Saints (continued)

(c) Gather us into communion with (*N* and) all your saints;
nourish and strengthen us in the life of heaven,
and confirm us in the faith and truth of Christ.

EUCHARISTIC PRAYER 3

The Lord be with you *or* The Lord is here.
and also with you. **His Spirit is with us.**

Lift up your hearts.
We lift them to the Lord.

Let us give thanks to the Lord our God.
It is right to give him thanks and praise.

Blessed are you, Lord, God of the universe,
you bring forth bread from the earth.
Blessed be God for ever.
Blessed are you, Lord, God of the universe,
you create the fruit of the vine.
Blessed be God for ever.
The whole universe praises you, its creator.
Sun and rain, hills and rivers praise you.
Blessed be God for ever.
The fruit of the earth itself praises you:
Wheat and grape, this bread and wine,
are part of the riches of your earth.
You are worthy, our Lord and God,
to receive glory and honour and power,
for you created all things,
and through your will they have their being.

You made us in your image,
and were faithful even when we turned against you.
You loved us so much you gave up your Son to die
that we might no longer be slaves to sin
but rise to life with him.

(A proper preface may be inserted here)

Earth unites with heaven to sing the new song of creation
as we adore and praise you for ever, saying
Holy, holy, holy Lord,
God of power and might,
Heaven and earth are full of your glory.
Hosanna in the highest!

**(Blessed is he who comes in the name of the Lord.
Hosanna in the highest!)**

Until he comes in glory
we keep the feast that Jesus began.
At supper with his friends on the night he was betrayed
He took bread and gave you thanks.
He broke it and gave it to them, saying:
'Take, eat. This is my body, given for you.'

At the end of supper, taking the cup of wine,
he gave you thanks, and said:
'Drink this, all of you;
This is my blood of the new covenant,
shed for you and for many for the forgiveness of sins.
Do this in remembrance of me.'

We eat and drink;
We proclaim his death today;
We celebrate his offering of himself
once for all on the cross,
his resurrection, ascension and coming again:

We proclaim your mighty acts
**You chose us to be your people
You made us a royal priesthood
We offer you the sacrifice of praise.**

or

Praise to you, Lord Jesus.
**Dying you destroyed our death
Rising you restored our life
Lord Jesus, come in glory!**

We are your own creation in Christ:
Fill us with your Spirit
to bring good news to the poor,
to heal the broken-hearted,
to announce release to captives
and freedom to prisoners.
As we eat this bread and drink this wine:
**Come, Holy Spirit,
fill our sacrifice of praise and thanksgiving
with your power and love.**

Unite us with your church throughout the world
as we join the song of heaven:

**Worthy is the Lamb that was sacrificed,
to receive power and wealth, wisdom and might,
honour and glory and praise! Amen.**

EUCHARISTIC PRAYER 4

The Lord be with you *or* The Lord is here.
and also with you. **His Spirit is with us.**

Lift up your hearts.
We lift them to the Lord.

Let us give thanks to the Lord our God.
It is right to give him thanks and praise.

Lord God of justice and mercy,
you care for the world and for every child of your creation;
we glorify your Name.
You call us to share your life and you give us your love.
You are our Father, kind and gentle,
always ready to forgive.
You delight in our joy, listen patiently to our troubles,
and comfort us in distress.
(Therefore with the whole company of heaven
we proclaim your great and glorious name,
for ever praising you and saying)
Holy, holy, holy Lord,
God of power and might,
Heaven and earth are full of your glory.
Hosanna in the highest!

(Blessed is he who comes in the name of the Lord.
Hosanna in the highest!)

Father we glorify your Name for ever.
(We glorify your Name for ever).

Though created in your image, we rebelled against you,
but you show your love in Jesus Christ your Word made flesh.
He is your Good News to the world; through him we are saved.
He suffered for our sake
and gave up his life on the cross to be a ransom for many.
(Crucified Lord, we praise you.)

In the upper room with his friends
on the night on which he was betrayed,
Jesus took bread and gave you thanks.
He broke it and gave it to them, saying:
'Take, eat. This is my body, given for you.'

At the end of supper, taking the cup of wine,
he gave you thanks, and said:
'Drink this, all of you;
This is my blood of the new covenant,
shed for you and for many for the forgiveness of sins.
Do this in remembrance of me.'
(Jesus, you are the true vine).

God of all holiness, we are gathered in your Name
to celebrate the one sacrifice Jesus made for us all,
and to praise you for his glorious resurrection.
By your Spirit may these gifts of bread and wine
be for us Christ's body and blood;
as we do this in remembrance of him,
may we feed on him by faith with thanksgiving.
(Holy Spirit, you are the Power of God.)

Lord of all life, help us to work together for your kingdom,
and for that day when your justice and mercy
will be seen in all the world.
By your grace unite us in Christ with your whole Church
on earth and in heaven,
so that with one voice we may worship you
and praise your Name:

**Blessing and honour and glory and power,
be yours for ever and ever. Amen**

EUCHARISTIC PRAYER 5

The Lord be with you *or* The Lord is here.
and also with you. **His Spirit is with us.**

Lift up your hearts.
We lift them to the Lord.

Let us give thanks to the Lord our God.
It is right to give him thanks and praise.

*(Here the President leads the thanksgiving
for God's mighty acts in creation and redemption.
This form or another must be used. See the Appendix for examples)*

Father, you made the world and love your creation.
Through Jesus Christ your Son, our Lord,

we give you thanks and praise.
His dying and rising have set us free from sin and death.
By your Spirit you make us your friends.

Therefore we join the saints and angels
and sing together,
Holy, holy, holy Lord,
God of power and might,
Heaven and earth are full of your glory.
Hosanna in the highest!

(Blessed is he who comes in the name of the Lord.
Hosanna in the highest!)

Praise and thanks to you, Father in heaven:
on the night on which he was betrayed
your Son Jesus Christ took bread and gave you thanks
he broke it and gave it to his disciples, saying:
'This is my body, given for you.'
Taking the cup of wine, he said: 'This is my blood,
shed for you and for many for the forgiveness of sins.
Do this in remembrance of me.'

As we remember his death on the cross,
his sacrifice once for all to save us
we rejoice in his living presence.

(Great is the mystery of faith:)
Christ has died.
Christ is risen.
Christ will come again.

Send your Holy Spirit,
that the bread which we break
and the cup which we bless
may be the communion of the body and blood of Christ.

Unite us with him
and with all God's people in heaven and earth.
Glory, worship, praise and thanksgiving
be to you, our God, Father, Son and Holy Spirit,
for ever and ever. Amen.

An alternative doxology may be sung.

APPENDIX

1
Father, we give you thanks
through Jesus Christ your Son, our Lord
and praise his holy name:

Jesus, Lord of all creation,
we worship and adore you.

Jesus, born as one of us,
we worship and adore you.

Jesus, your death has set us free,
we worship and adore you.

Jesus, raised to life again,
we worship and adore you.

Jesus, reigning in glory now,
we worship and adore you.

2
Father, we give you thanks
through Jesus Christ your Son, our Lord
and praise his holy name:

Jesus, Son of God,
we worship and adore you.

Jesus, our friend and brother,
we worship and adore you.

Jesus, light of all the world,
we worship and adore you.

Jesus, our way, our truth, our life,
we worship and adore you.

Jesus, Lord of all,
we worship and adore you.

Jesus, bread of heaven,
we worship and adore you.

3 Christmas
God of all glory, we give you thanks,
through Jesus Christ your Son our Lord
and praise his holy name:

Heavenly King, born of Mary;
God of all glory
we worship and adore you.

Word of the Father, crying as a little child;
God of all glory
we worship and adore you.

Robed in high majesty, wrapped in
infant clothes;
God of all glory
we worship and adore you.

3 Christmas (continued)
Lord of heaven and earth, laid in a manger;
God of all glory
we worship and adore you.
Strong in weakness,
glorious in humility,
to him be all praise and glory.
We join with all the company
of heaven, saying...

4 Cross
We give you thanks and praise,
God of all glory,
through Jesus Christ your Son our Lord.

He was betrayed, deserted by his friends.
In our world of treachery and loneliness
God of all glory
we worship and adore you.

Though he was innocent, he was tried and
condemned,
scorned and ill-treated.
In our world of hatred and injustice
God of all glory
we worship and adore you.

He was publicly put to death
with nails through hands and feet.
In our world of brutality and pain
God of all glory
we worship and adore you.

On the cross he won the victory
over sin and death for ever.
In our world of desolation and despair
God of all glory
we worship and adore you.

We worship and adore you for the glory
of the cross,
here on earth and in the glory of heaven,
with angels and archangels:

5 Resurrection
We give you thanks and praise,
God of all glory,
through Jesus Christ your Son our Lord.
He was crucified, dead and buried,
laid in a tomb
but death could not hold him.
God of all glory
we worship and adore you.

5 Resurrection (continued)
You raised him to life as you promised,
to the amazement of Mary and
Peter and John.
God of all glory
we worship and adore you.

He met and talked with his disciples
in the upper room and on the seashore.
God of all glory
we worship and adore you.

We have been crucified with Christ
and live with him the risen life.
God of all glory
we worship and adore you.

So on earth and in heaven for ever
we praise you with angels and archangels:

6 Resurrection
Praise be to you, our Father,
for your Son Jesus Christ.
He lived and died for love of us,
and, after rising from the dead,
yet more wonderfully met with his
disciples.
He walked with them,
taught them about you,
and shared supper with them.

EUCHARISTIC PRAYER 6

The Lord be with you
and also with you.

or

The Lord is here.
His Spirit is with us.

Lift up your hearts.
We lift them to the Lord.

Let us give thanks to the Lord our God.
It is right to give him thanks and praise.

Heavenly Father, we give you thanks and praise
through Jesus Christ your Son our Lord.
For he is your living Word;
through him you have created all things from the beginning,
and have formed us in your own image.

**You are worthy, O Lord our God,
to receive glory and honour and power.
For you created all things,
and by your will they have their being.**

We praise you through Jesus Christ your Son
because you have given him to be born as man
and to die upon the cross for us.
We praise you for raising him from the dead
and exalting him to your right hand on high.
So we join the saints and angels, and sing together:
**Holy, holy, holy Lord,
God of power and might,
Heaven and earth are full of your glory.
Hosanna in the highest!**

**(Blessed is he who comes in the name of the Lord.
Hosanna in the highest!)**

And now, heavenly Father, we pray that at this supper,
as we follow his example and obey his command,
your gifts of bread and wine
may by the power of the Spirit be to us his body and his blood.

**Worthy is the Lamb, the Lamb who was slain
to receive power and wealth and wisdom and strength
and honour and glory and praise.**

For on the night that he was betrayed,
Jesus took bread and gave you thanks.
He broke it and gave it to his disciples, saying:
'Take, eat. This is my body, given for you.'

At the end of supper, taking the cup of wine,
he gave you thanks, and said:
'Drink this, all of you;
This is my blood of the new covenant,
shed for you and for many for the forgiveness of sins.
Do this in remembrance of me.'

**As often as we eat this bread and drink this cup
we proclaim the death of the Lord until he comes.**

Therefore, heavenly Father, we remember his death,
his offering of himself made once for all upon the cross,
and we proclaim his mighty resurrection and glorious ascension,
keeping his feast until he comes again.

**Christ has died
Christ is risen
Christ will come again.**

Father, we give you thanks and praise
that through him you have sent upon us
your holy and life-giving Spirit
and made us a people for your own possession,

**Father, grant that by your Holy Spirit
we may feed on Christ
and be strengthened for your service.**

All glory and praise be yours
in Jesus Christ and through your Holy Spirit
as we join the endless praise of heaven:

**Blessing and honour and glory and power
be yours for ever and ever. Amen.**

5

Eucharists When Children are Present: Pastoral Issues and Suggestions

Issues

We list first four issues for discussion in the PCC or Parish Worship Group when questions about children and eucharistic worship are being considered. Then we offer suggestions for eucharistic worship when children are present.

1 The Context

The problem about producing one or two Eucharistic Prayers suitable for use when children are present is that there is a wide range of different expectations from the same textual material. The Roman Catholics distinguish between 'children's masses in which only a few adults participate' and 'adult masses in which children participate.' Some of the services in the first category will be school eucharists, some of them will be in school, while others may be in church. The number of children participating in the sense of receiving communion will be very different in an Anglican context, as may be the amount of integration into the overall life of the school. And in some ways there is a continuum, rather than a clear distinction between these two categories. At one end might be a weekday service in a school hall, or a Sunday service in a family service idiom, where much of the worship is geared for children, and at the other a service in which there may be only a few children present, but it is important not to neglect them. The Roman Catholic 'Directory on Children's Masses' says of this, 'care must be taken not to allow the children to feel neglected because of their inability to participate in and understand what is being done and proclaimed in the celebration. At the very least some account must be taken of their presence; for example, by saying a special word to them at the beginning and at the end of the Mass and in some part of the Homily.'

2 A 'Half-way House'?

Are these services a 'bridge' into more 'adult' worship, or are they the main diet for the congregation every Sunday? There will be some who will see such services, whether in school or church, as a preparation for involvement in more 'adult' or traditional worship. Some will argue that in such a situation, more flexibility should be allowed, to truncate the structure or major on a particular teaching theme by rewriting parts of the Eucharistic Prayer. This would seem to point to the need for a recognized amount of flexibility in both structure and in eucharistic prefaces or variables. We can see some advantage in occasionally having an 'animateur,' deacon or commentator to explain the service as it proceeds. It is important that this is done with a lightness of touch, and not by the president. Care should be taken over the position (and the dress?) of such an 'animateur:' the lectern should be reserved for the Word of God, the pulpit in some places may be suitable, but in others may be too dominant or encourage a preaching approach; a position to one side or walking about may be best, avoiding a central position which might create confusion as to who is taking the action forward. There will be a distinction between such educational activity and the main text of the service, and those responsible for worship should resist the temptation to introduce educational themes and words into the text. The celebration of the eucharist is primarily a time for worship rather than for education.

But there will be others who will want to use these prayers in a main Sunday service, when there are numbers of children and families present every Sunday. Care should be taken in planning such all-age activities, that the needs of adults, including the elderly and those who do not fit into the 'family' image, are taken seriously. The same prayer could not be used every Sunday: there is deliberately a variety of prayers here, some more suitable for older young people and adults. Traditional texts should also be regularly used, so that there is a creative interplay between the two.

3 Children and Adults Relating Together

We believe that it is important that the needs of both these categories, the 'bridge,' often in a context where there are large numbers of children present, and the intermittent use of such prayers in a main Sunday service, are met by the same group of Eucharistic Prayers. Our baptism marks us out as members of the one Body of Christ. It is as members of that body that we come together for worship, recognizing the presence and absence of other members of that body in space and time. Our eucharistic worship, uniting us as it does not only with angels and archangels but with slaughtered infants and geriatric saints, is not the place to divide the Christian community on the basis of age. So while some of these prayers may seem fairly simple, they still contain an element of mystery (and some words with a spiritual depth we are unwilling to simplify), and also the possibility of that kind of seasonal and thematic variety which opens the door to some biblical richness of imagery. Though some of these prayers, in structure and language, may seem more suitable for younger, and some more suitable for older children or adults, we believe that all of them should be capable of use by the whole church, without having a specific age label attached. There must be scope for spiritual growth through the liturgy, and all of us, not just the children, need to grow into a deeper appreciation of what lies behind words like 'kingdom,' 'grace,' 'sacrifice,' 'ransom' and 'remembrance:' it is not sufficient simply to have a superficial knowledge of them, and in this way adults and children are in the same boat. In the praying of these prayers adults need to learn from children, and children from adults, as part of the same Body.

4 The Need for Flexibility

The RC *Directory on Children's Masses* has a system of permissible adaptations:

> 'The general structure of the Mass...must always remain unchanged. However, in order that children, in their own way and in accordance with the laws of child psychology, may genuinely experience "the mystery of faith...through the rites and prayers," the undermentioned adaptations in the different parts of the celebration would seem to be necessary.'

While there are some things which should never be adapted, such as the Lord's Prayer and the Trinitarian formula which concludes the blessing, there are many others which are open to adaptation, such as the content of the opening rite, the number of readings (which may be reduced to one), the Creed, and even the text of the Eucharistic Prayer: 'the text of the Roman Missal prayers may be adapted to their needs, but the purpose and substance of these prayers should be preserved.' This last provision was withdrawn by the Holy See after the Eucharistic Prayers for Children were brought out, but it is some indication of a more flexible approach than our own.

How far should the Church of England should be open to such permissible adaptations for worship when children are present? The provision for *A Service of the Word* to be combined with Holy Communion opens the door to a certain amount of flexibility, within a framework which can be close to Rite A or more like a 'Family Service:'

- a variety of ways of beginning the service is spelt out in Note 1
- far greater variety is now provided in authorized confessions and absolutions, some of them responsive in form
- Notes 5 and 7 give encouragement to alternative ways of presenting readings and sermon
- the collect may be included within the intercessions
- an authorized Affirmation of Faith (again including responsive and shorter forms) may replace the Creed and neither need be used on weekdays.

Eucharistic Prayers and the Eucharist: Some Suggestions

We believe that it is not possible to isolate the Eucharistic Prayer from the rest of the service. The way in which this is planned and led is at least as important as the text of the Eucharistic Prayers themselves. The Liturgical Commission is concerned with the whole area of liturgical formation and presentation, and not simply with texts. Therefore, we offer some guidelines, section by section, on the liturgical context in which these new Eucharistic Prayers will be used. And in line with our view of the unity of the worshipping community ('children are people, not a different sort of animal,' someone said), we would expect many of these questions and suggestions to reflect good practice for adults too. Much will depend on the particular context, the proportion of children present, whether the service is on a weekday or a Sunday, and the worshipping experience of the local congregation.

1 Planning and Preparing
- Involve children, for example in choosing hymns and songs.
- Involve them in the production of music, drama, movement, dance, visual materials, artwork or computer production of a service sheet.
- Plan to use Sunday School work from the previous Sunday.
- Preparing the worship room or church and producing any special decorations (for example round the pillars or at the entrance, or a collage-type temporary altar frontal or banners).
- Preparing chalice, paten etc.
- Preparing biddings or prayers for the intercessions.
- Preparing the insertion of reasons for giving thanks before the Preface.

When the planning is complete, it is important to ask whether the major climaxes and the eucharistic action are still clear, whether the balance is right between teaching and worship, between words to the congregation and words to God.

2 Gathering
- What is the best place for children to sit? Together or with their families? How much can they see and feel part of the action?
- How do children come into church? Should some be part of the welcome team? Should some be servers, entering with the president and being in the sanctuary?
- Should some or all of the children come in with the president, to help them realize that they are forming themselves into the Eucharistic community?
- If children come back into church (say from Sunday School) during the service, should they enter (quietly ignored?) during a hymn, or should their entrance be marked in some way? What might they contribute at this point from what they have been doing—a song, banner or word to a parent during the Peace?

3 Confession
- Use a simpler introduction to confession, followed by silence.
- Use a short responsive form, with the same response, such as those in *A Service of the Word*. There are examples of the Kyrie form in *The Promise of His Glory* and *Patterns for Worship*.
- Vary the absolution, sometimes using a simpler form than the highly theological *ASB* text. Again, some of those in *A Service of the Word* are suitable.

4 Readings

It is still necessary to have at least two readings at the Eucharist, one of which must be the Gospel, and both of which must come from the Lectionary. Some readings might need some abbreviation, or careful introduction, if there are numbers of children present. Variety in the presentation of the Ministry of the Word is important. Consider:

- A dramatic reading, written for several voices with narrator and characters as for instance in the *Dramatized Bible*.
- A reading from the Bible with visual accompaniment. This might involve mime, tableau, drama, dance or puppets (shadow puppets are more easily seen by large numbers). There might be projected slides or OHP transparencies of the story drawn by the children.
- The Gospel might be read and either preceded or followed by a free adaptation, for instance in dialogue form, transposing it to a modern setting.
- A reading backed with appropriate music.
- A dramatic reading with people speaking from different parts of the church.
- Carefully rehearsed choral speaking by a group.

5 The Sermon

Note 7 in *A Service of the Word* makes clear that this term includes 'less formal exposition, the use of drama, interviews, discussion and audio-visuals.' Dialogue with children might form part of the sermon, and there is scope here for imaginative inter-generational activity.

The sermon may come at different points in the service, either after one of the readings or before or after the prayers, and it may be in a number of different sections, with hymns or parts of the service inserted.

6 The Intercessions

Again, there are different ways of involving children and families in these:

- Use prayers or biddings written by children; they might or might not read them, or might read biddings with an adult praying.
- Write a special litany with the children contributing. This could be prepared beforehand, or compiled as children arrive at the start of the service.
- Use a poster, or a few projected slides or overhead transparencies drawn by the children as a focus for prayer, either in silence or with some corporate response.
- Put a previously prepared collage representing prayer needs in a prominent position.
- Use a list of prayer topics or biddings with time for silent reflection.
- Any form of visual stimulus such as mime or tableaux could be followed by prayer and response.
- Prayers may be sung, entirely or with sung responses composed by the children.
- Pray informally in small inter-generational groups.

7 The Peace

Some thought should be given to the method of exchanging the Peace when there are numbers of children present. Is a solemn handshake right for small children? Is it easier if it is a more ritualized action? Is there a danger of children getting overlooked when, for example, the adults are doing a lot of hugging? Can children take the initiative in exchanging the Peace? Other ways of doing it may be possible from time to time, for instance joining hands in a large circle or presenting some word or token to one another.

8 The Eucharistic Prayers

The only Eucharistic Prayers which are authorized for Church of England use are those in the *BCP* or approved by the General Synod under Canon B2. This includes those in the *ASB* but not the ones in this booklet, the RC prayers, or any others which might have been locally permitted. Bishops have no power to authorize Eucharistic Prayers.

Various factors will enter into the choice of the Eucharistic Prayer for a particular service:

- The age and Christian experience of the congregation
- The season of the year or the theme of the service
- The need to balance the benefit of security which the regular use of one prayer brings with the benefit of exploring the richness of our eucharistic tradition which might come with a variety of prayers. It is particularly important, in terms of regular Sunday use, to use some of the more adult prayers, and those of a more traditional pattern from time to time.
- Brevity should not be the only criterion.

There are a number of ways of presenting the Eucharistic Prayer which, used sparingly, might help children and adults.

- With a small congregation, it might be possible to come and stand around the table for the Eucharistic Prayer.
- In some churches, children (and others) might copy the actions of the president, for instance in raising hands during the dialogue.
- Some changing visual background might be used, for example projecting slides onto a screen behind the president, or having children raise banners which mark the different actions in the pattern of the eucharist.
- Music might be used, not only in the traditional places, but to insert songs, responses or a reflective instrumental piece within the prayer; and in the traditional items, such as the Sanctus, a musical form might be repetitive.
- Consider preambles before the Eucharistic Prayer. This might be a set of biddings or reasons for giving thanks, spoken by children or others, before or after the opening dialogue. For longer preambles, there are examples in the Maundy Thursday Service in *Lent, Holy Week, Easter*, and Eucharistic Prayer 3 in this collection. Jewish-style questions and answers such as those overleaf might be compiled, perhaps to echo the theme of the service. A child might ask the questions, which might be answered by president or deacon, and not all questions need be attempted every time.

Q Why do we give thanks and praise to God?
A Because he has created all that is, and he has given us life. He is Lord of all, and yet loves each of us.
Q Why do we remember Jesus?
A Because he was sent from God and he gave up his life for us on the cross. God raised him from the dead so that we might see that death is not the end, but the beginning of a new life, the life Jesus showed us how to live.
Q Why do we use bread?
A Because Jesus took bread at the Last Supper. It is a sign of Jesus feeding us as we share with others around his table.
Q Why do we use wine?
A Because this wine, poured out, is a sign of Jesus' saving love for us as we walk with him along the path of new life.

The actions, style and approach of the president, while being accessible to children, should make clear that the whole prayer is addressed to God, in whose presence it is right to be filled with awe. The sense of mystery should not lose out to a chatty educational or instructional approach.

9 The Communion

Those children who do not receive communion are in the difficult position of being fully part of the Body of Christ, the worshipping community, perhaps having an increased level of participation and yet not taking part in the climax of the service. Where many are not communicants, the words at the breaking of the bread, '…we are one body, because we all share in one bread' may be inappropriate, and we have suggested alternative sets of words. For some children the communion can be long and boring, a poor preparation for their eventual joyful participation. Where practicable, each child should be blessed (not necessarily by a priest) with a suitable form of words. Some suggestions can be found on page 225 of *Patterns*. It is not appropriate to give children chocolate buttons or blessed bread in the context of the eucharist.

Some children may be able to help, in the sanctuary, or as ushers, or in a music or singing group. But most will need some help, perhaps through parents and Sunday School leaders and suitable literature, to use this time profitably, especially if there is silence. Children will learn by watching, catching the atmosphere from the movements and attitude of those who distribute and the communicants.

10 Post-communion

In a service where a large number do not receive communion, the standard Rite A post-communion prayer (Section 53) sounds rather false, and might be replaced by that at Section 86 or by one of the post-communion prayers in *Patterns*. A prayer may be used which sums up the theme for the day.

Suggestions under 'Gathering' above may also apply to leaving church.

6
Commentary on the Six Prayers

The first two prayers are the two returned to the Synod by the House of Bishops in November 1994. The one thing they have in common is that, unlike the others, each started life in a RC draft text. Prayer 1 was drafted for the Commission in 1992, using about 25 lines from the proposed text of the Eucharistic Prayers 1, 2 and 3 for masses with children which were then being evaluated by ICEL. 'Hosanna in the highest,' for example, is taken from the first of these. This prayer was 'field-tested' and the subsequent video was shown at a consultation with Diocesan Liturgical Committees, and the prayer was modified as a result.

The lines about creation in the early part of the Thanksgiving have undergone many changes. One of the problems has been to find words which are acceptable in both town and country, and also relate to the human creation. The proposal that these lines might be replaced with other lines of similar length, in the note at the end of the prayer, is one which it would have been good to test out. The ending of the prayer was changed in the Revision Committee, to provide congregational doxologies, introduced by a strong trinitarian reference. As in all the other prayers, the convention has been adopted of placing the Benedictus within brackets. Clearly, this prayer is capable of many different uses: the video showed that music in the responses can help participation, especially for children.

Prayer 2 owes its origin to 'Original eucharistic prayer, Text 1,' published by ICEL in 1984, but considerably changed. The unnecessary split invocation of the Spirit has gone. The treatment of sacrifice in the memorial is quite different. But the vivid use of paradox in the original has been retained—phrases such as 'silent music,' used by John of the Cross and recently by Pasternak. The feminine image of 'as a mother tenderly gathers her children' has also been criticized, though it reflects the picture of God's gathering of his people from Isaiah 66.13 and Matthew 23.37. The major innovation is the use of optional insertions at three points.

In the anamnesis—epiclesis the Commission proposed to test two words. The word 'plead' has survived through the revision process. It has been used by evangelicals and Calvinists, and is also used of the eucharist in the answer to Leo XIII's Bull against Anglican Orders by the Anglican Archbishops in 1897. The balance in the phrase 'Plead with confidence,' with the stress on the once for all sacrifice, links with the Johannine paradoxical phrase 'dying and rising in glory' and with the intercession of Christ in heaven. The coming of the Spirit flows directly from that. Here, and in Prayer 4, the word 'show' did not survive the revision process. The pictorial 'pour out' has survived, though the reference to the Holy Spirit being poured 'out over these gifts' has gone.

Prayer 3, with its use of texts from Revelation 4 and 5, sets the action in heaven. The opening blessings echo the Jewish table prayers and also the 'Benedicite.' If the earlier part of the prayer is rooted in creation, the clyst-narrative section, echoing

Isaiah 61, roots it in the city and in the purpose of the church, bringing good news, healing and release. During the revision process the structure of the prayer was simplified, the proper prefaces omitted and the innovative style brought nearer to the standard 'received' pattern.

Prayer 4, originally drafted by a secondary school teacher and an English expert, has a very clear Trinitarian structure, with single-line responses, one for each person of the Trinity and for bread and wine. The structure brings together creation and redemption with echoes from the prophets of a God of 'justice and mercy.' The redemption theme was heightened by the Revision Committee in the sequence of creation-rebellion-redemption. The use of the present tense here is intentional, and is part of the Commission's view of the contemporary results of the historic action of God reflected in the eucharistic prayer. The post-narrative paragraph, combining anamnesis and epiclesis, through the prayer for the Spirit moves on to the task of the church and the eschatological hope for justice and mercy, neatly bringing the prayer back to where it began.

Prayer 5 was produced during revision by a Group appointed by the Commission and the Board of Education, which produced a set of principles for the construction of such prayers. It is based partly on one in use in ecumenical circles, and also draws in part on the discarded Prayer 1 from GS1120, the shortest of the original prayers. A main feature is the rubric: '*Here the President leads the thanksgiving for God's mighty acts in creation and redemption.*' A brief form for presidential thanksgiving appears in the text, with various sample responsive forms in the appendix; this clearly allows for the thanksgiving to be produced locally. However, it should not be used on a regular basis. This kind of flexible approach within a clear structure, much welcomed by those in the education world, is one which it would have been good to try out officially across the whole church; and it might have succeeded in discouraging people from inventing complete eucharistic prayers.

Prayer 6 came from the Revision Committee. It was not, however, innovative, but was in continuity with the First Eucharistic Prayer in Rite A and was deliberately intended to be a principled development from that Prayer. Thus the epiclesis is placed as in that Prayer—a point at which this prayer is distinctive within the new six—illustrating that there is still sympathy for prayers of the Rite A sort amongst those drafting and authorizing new prayers built on more radical lines.

Once that continuity with Rite A is grasped, then the prayer is best described by the points at which it has responded to criticisms of Rite A, thus:.

1. The prayer is shortened yet made more responsive. The First Prayer had 14 congregational lines (out of its 74): this prayer has 26 (out of its 63).
2. The structure of the prayer has been made more overtly Trinitarian, even though retaining the 'Western' epiclesis.
3. A more logical sequence has been developed after the narrative of institution. The Acclamations in Rite A come too early in the developing story. A well-known sacramental text (1 Cor 11.26) responds to the narrative, whilst the anamnesis following leads more naturally into the existing Acclamations.